SOUTHWESTERN INDIAN WEAVING

by Mark Bahti
photography by Bruce Hucko

Mark Bahti has been in the Indian arts business for over 30 years. During that time he has also pursued an academic interest in cross-cultural communication, and been involved in a number of urban Indian issues ranging from employment to education.

Bruce Hucko—photographer, writer, educator, and children's art coach—focuses on themes of community, art, landscape, and people, and their interrelationships.

Special Thanks to the artists and the following institutions for their help:
Bahti Indian Arts, Burnham Trading Post, Janice and Joe Day of Tsakurshovi, Hubbell Trading Post National Historic Site, Jicarilla Apache Tribal Co-op, Oke Okweenge Co-op, Sacred Mountain Trading Post, Adam and Harriett Simons Collection, TOCA Basketweavers, Twin Rocks Trading Post, Wetherill Grand Gulch Research Project.

INDEX

Song of the Sky Loom

O our Mother the Earth, O our Father the Sky
Your children are we, and with tired backs
We bring you the gifts that you love.
Then weave for us a garment of brightness;
May the warp be the white light of morning,
May the weft be the red light of evening,
May the fringes be the falling rain,
May the border be the standing rainbow,
Thus weave for us a garment of brightness
That we may walk fittingly where the birds sing,
That we may walk fittingly where grass is green,
O our Mother the Earth, O our Father the Sky!

TEWA PRAYER TRANSLATED BY HERBERT SPINDEN—*Songs of the Tewa*

In the Beginning

Woven bags from the ancient Pueblo peoples ranged from very finely woven and dyed textiles to more quickly woven, utilitarian pieces like this yucca fiber bag found in southwestern Colorado.

Prehistoric weaving traditions in the Southwest, which evolved over thousands of years, were rich and varied. Despite the ravages of time and pothunting, several thousand prehistoric textile specimens have been recovered from the Greater Southwest. Using many variations of six basic methods of weaving—interlacing, twining, crossing and recrossing, wrapping, looping, and linking—prehistoric weavers in the Southwest created a dizzying array of woven objects including mats; cordage; twine; straps; sandals; storage, gathering, parching, winnowing, water, and cooking baskets; shirts; carrying bags; leggings; garters; dresses; skirts; belts; sashes; kilts; and breechcloths.

Colors were dyed-in, resist-dyed, tie-dyed (A.D. 110), painted (A.D. 900), and stamped (A.D. 1100). Colors used by these early weavers included red, yellow, blue, purple, black, brown/black, brown, green, yellow-brown, purplish red, orange, and pink. Cochineal, a dye derived from an insect, is most commonly mentioned as the only source of red, and indigo—a plant dye—as the only source of blue, but in fact there were other sources, including lac (another insect) for red and red clover for blue. Murex and purpura shells were a source for purple, and copper oxide for blue-green.

The range of materials used was equally impressive in its inventiveness and diversity. Those used included agave, yucca, milkweed, willow, juniper bark, sotol, bear grass, hemp, mesquite, human hair, animal fur—including bison, bighorn sheep, and domesticated dog—rabbit skin strips (the fur is too fine to be spun itself so strips were woven around yucca fiber cores), turkey feathers, and finally, cotton.

USE OF COTTON

Cotton (*Gossypium hirsutum*) was domesticated in Mexico—perhaps as early as 3,000 B.C. according to some estimates—and introduced to groups further north between A.D. 100 and 500. With the new material came a new weaving technology—the backstrap belt loom and upright or

These ancient Pueblo sandals of twined yucca fiber date back to Basketmaker II. They were found in the proposed San Juan-Anasazi Wilderness area and were left where they were found, allowing others the opportunity to experience the same excitement of discovery.

While the Navajo weaving tradition continues strong, elements of it are undergoing change. Time pressures combined with a market that does not recompense weavers for added time and skill are causing weavers to discontinue using hand-spun wool in favor of processed and commercially spun wool. Hazel Tallman is one of a declining number of weavers who still use hand-spun (also called "homespun") wool.

This assemblage of ancient Pueblo-woven carrying bags, pouches, and basketry containers—demonstrating a wide range of weaving techniques—was found in the Mesa Verde region of southwestern Colorado.

vertical loom. The people of Hohokam and Mogollon cultures—closer to Mesoamerican cultures than were the northern Puebloan peoples—were among the first to begin growing and weaving cotton. Along with the design motifs came the cultural beliefs associated with them. Among the Nahuatl Indians in Mexico, Xochiquetzal—the first woman, and the patroness of spinning and weaving—was also associated with fertility and rain or water, which in turn is connected with water serpents. The serpent cult of ancient Mexico begins to appear in the Southwest about the same time that cotton does.

By A.D. 700 cotton was being cultivated in the major Southwest desert drainage areas. It was introduced in the northern pueblos as a cultivated crop by A.D. 1100. Archaeological evidence indicates that it was a major, valuable trade item.

Though most of the trade was in raw cotton, exceptional textiles were also traded, with Hopi

Durable willow baskets woven by the Pima and Apache Indians of the Southwest continued to be woven to be used for storage, gathering, carrying, winnowing, parching, and trade well into the 1900s. Today the craft has nearly disappeared among both tribes.

6

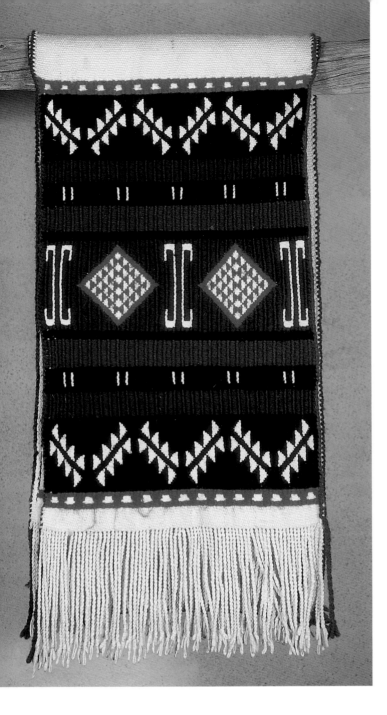

fabrics achieving widespread distribution. Among the Hopi, women historically handled trade in textiles between and within the Hopi villages, while long-distance trade was handled by the men. As late as the Spanish era, Pueblo Indians from the Zuni to the people of Taos were trading for raw cotton and finished textiles from the Hopi. Even the Opas, a Yuman people along the lower Colorado, traded with the Hopi for cotton and cotton textiles even though the Pima along the Gila River were much closer.

While at Hopi the men were the weavers, this was not necessarily the case in other pueblos. An early ethnologist at Zuni reported in the 1880s that Zuni men and women wove. She wrote of a young Zuni boy, about 12 years old, who wove a double saddle blanket to show her that the Zuni could weave as well as the Navajo.

The Hopi were prolific weavers. An early Spanish military leader records having received many hundreds of textiles—primarily blankets and mantas—in payment of tribute just from the two Hopi villages on First Mesa. Yet records from the same era acknowledge that a one-textile-per-person annual tribute from the Rio Grande pueblos could not be met.

This Hopi dance sash from Second Mesa is an important part of the clothing worn by many Hopi katsinas. It is the need for religious articles of clothing that has kept Pueblo weaving traditions (which at Hopi are practiced solely by the men) alive and vital. There is a strong intertribal trade for Pueblo textiles.

Willow water baskets—one covered with pinyon pitch and the other as it looks before the pitch is applied. This type of basket was used by a number of tribes, including the Ute, Paiute, Navajo, and Apache for carrying water. Long since replaced by metal containers and indoor plumbing, they are still made—both for collectors and as a way to keep a part of the old ways alive.

In this scene from a San Ildefonso Harvest Dance—taken with prior approval—the vital role of Pueblo textiles in the modern life of the village can be seen. The women wear black mantas lightly embroidered in red and green and belted with a red, green, and black sash, while the men wear white rain sashes, embroidered kilts, and anklets while taking part in the religious life of the pueblo.

VARYING DEMAND

The demand for specialized clothing for religious observances has kept the weaving tradition alive. Contemporary textile production among the pueblos continues today. Where it has largely disappeared in some pueblos, others produce textiles for "export" to these and other pueblos. Currently Hopi has the most active weaving tradition among the pueblos. Kilts, belts, ceremonial dance sashes, rain sashes, black mantas, white mantas, and embroidered mantas, as well as knitted and crocheted leggings, are still made by the men of Hopi, though a few women have begun to provide the knitted and crocheted items.

Demand for clothing for religious purposes has kept embroidered fabric traditions as well as some limited weaving alive in other pueblos as well. The craft cooperative at San Juan Pueblo, Oke Okweenge, was established in 1970 in part to keep the tradition of embroidered textiles alive. Such work from San Juan finds its way into virtually every other pueblo. Embroiderers from Laguna can see their work at Hopi, and works of Hopi textile artists are worn at Zuni and among the Rio Grande pueblos. The trading networks of the prehistoric Southwest still hum with activity.

Additionally, a new market has arisen, with weavers producing works for secular fashion, worn by Indians and non-Indians alike. In the past century quilting, introduced by missionaries in the late 1800s, has also become a tradition in many Indian households. Change and innovation continue.

Quilt making was introduced among most tribes by missionaries. Among the Hopi, quilt making dates back to the late 1800s. This frog quilt is a recent example of work by Hopi quilters.

These embroidered dance kilts were made at San Juan Pueblo. The village cooperative, Oke Okweenge, has been the source for clothing used in Pueblo religious observances for decades. The work of San Juan artisans can be seen in virtually every single pueblo along the Rio Grande and as far west as the pueblos of Zuni, Acoma, and the Hopi villages.

The importance of textiles in Pueblo life cannot be overstated. While others may look at the designs in the kilts and sashes, trying to determine what each element may represent—clouds, rain, plants, sun—for the Pueblo peoples the importance, the significance lies in all the elements as they come together in vestments worn as a part of their traditional religious observances. Andrew Harvier of Santa Clara readies his daughter, KhaPovi, for participation in the village's annual Feast Day. Song, dance, prayer, and clothing combine to perform the religious ceremony.

9

Navajo Weaving

From ancient wearing apparel to the textile art of today, the history of Navajo weaving continues to be written, though many non-Navajo observers have predicted it will disappear in the next generation. Despite the doomsaying—some of those predictions are now more than a century old—there are more Navajo women weaving now than ever in the past. One expert places the number of current Navajo women weavers at close to 30,000. That said, the number of rugs an individual may weave in her lifetime *has* diminished. The demands of modern life no longer allow for the kind of time necessary to weave on a regular, continuing basis.

Though the quantity of weaving done for the market may have diminished, the value placed on the knowledge of weaving as a part of Navajo culture, of Navajo life, has not diminished. The time a young girl spends at the side of her mother, grandmother, or aunt is time in which she learns more than weaving—she learns about her culture, and in doing so, is woven into the fabric of Navajo life, Navajo tradition, and Navajo community—and becomes a part of the continuity of an evolving Navajo culture.

TRADITION

The *Diné* (dih NEH, meaning "the People"), who we know as the Navajo, are an Athabascan people who entered what is now North America some 25,000 years ago, eventually entering the land they now occupy a little over 600 years ago. According to the Navajo Creation Story, however, the Navajo have been in Dinétah, the Navajo homeland, since their emergence into this, the Fifth World.

Navajo weaver Jennie Slick demonstrates the vigorous use of a weaving comb in creating a tightly woven blanket. Many a Navajo infant has fallen asleep to the muffled thumping sound of a weaving comb as new yarns are woven in and the weaving advances upward.

This pattern with a corn stalk growing up from a ceremonial basket is typically called a "Tree of Life" after the form of a Mexican candelabra of the same name. It was woven by a member of the Nokadineh family, famous for their bird rugs.

Spider Rock in Canyon de Chelly figures prominently in Navajo legend surrounding Spider Woman. According to many versions, this stone formation, rising to dizzying heights from the canyon floor, was Spider Woman's home at the time she taught the first Navajo women how to weave. Canyon de Chelly was also once the home to Pueblo people—who anthropologists believe taught the Navajo how to weave.

These textiles represent the work of three generations in a weaving family. The grandmother (Rose Yazzie), who taught her daughters (Kara and Emily) to weave, is also teaching her granddaughters (Harriett and Carrie Whitney, and LaVera Blake). In a real-life reprise of the Navajo legend about Spider Woman teaching weaving to the Navajo, the grandmother lives in Canyon de Chelly, close to Spider Rock, and the girls have begun to be referred to as the Spider Rock Girls.

According to that same Navajo oral tradition, Spider Woman showed Navajo women how to weave on a loom constructed under the direction of Spider Man. The cross poles were made of earth and sky cords, the warps of sun rays, and the heddles of sheet lightning and rock crystal. Tools included a white shell comb, a batten made from the sun's halo, and finally, four spindle whorls: from the north zigzag lightning with a jet whorl, from the east a rain streamer with a white shell whorl, from the south sheet lightning with an abalone whorl, and from the west flash lightning with a turquoise whorl. The material with which they wove was wool—from churro sheep, which were given them at the time of Creation by Changing Woman.

According to ethnologists, Navajo weavers learned the craft from Pueblo weavers and used cotton early on (only one such example survives). It is generally thought that they learned the craft from weavers among the Pueblo people who fled from the anticipated Spanish retaliation after the Great Pueblo Revolt of 1680 to live among the Navajo, who had settled in the canyon country of the rugged San Juan Basin region in northwestern New Mexico. A nomadic people, the many different bands learned weaving at different times. The Navajo of Chaco Canyon, for example, have a legend that they learned weaving between 1675 and 1700 from a Pueblo woman—probably Zuni—whom they had taken in a raid.

With the scenic backdrop of the Hubbell Trading Post—site of many Navajo rug design revivals and innovations—are (left to right): a Third Phase Chief's blanket, a Second Phase Chief's blanket, and a woman's wearing blanket (an identification made solely upon size, not pattern). In the background are the corrals and barns that were a vital part of all trading posts. Navajo weaving was only one aspect of the trade at the Hubbell Trading Post and others like it; wool and livestock were the economic foundation.

SPANISH INFLUENCE

By the mid-1700s Navajo weavers had gained access to the wool from churro sheep brought by the Spanish settlers—mostly by gaining access to the sheep themselves through trading and raiding. The Navajo wove wearing blankets, hair ties, dresses, shirts, breechcloths, and leggings, as well as belts and sashes. Navajo women were highly-regarded weavers, and a number of Spanish households of the period had a Navajo woman, taken as a slave for the purpose of weaving. Early Spanish correspondence contains references to the outstanding quality of Navajo weaving and of its economic importance as a trade item.

Most of these early Navajo textiles were banded patterns in natural wool colors of white, gray, and dark brown. Indigo blue, a plant dye, was introduced to the region by the Spanish in the 1600s, along with cochineal red, derived from insect larvae. (The vegetal dyes many tend to think of as "traditional" were limited in use in early Navajo weaving, generally not used until the late 1800s.)

AMERICAN INFLUENCE

Navajo wearing blankets were highly regarded, much sought-after, and, predictably, rather expensive. An observer writing in 1844 stated that the best ones sold for as much as 50 to 60 dollars. Other writers, assuming that chiefs were the wealthy members of a band (a generally untrue assumption), began to call the predominant striped pattern a Chief's blanket. They were traded widely—several *hundred* Cheyenne women at Fort Bent, Colorado, had black and white striped "Chief's blankets," according to the post's trader.

Navajo weaving, valued for its usefulness, continued into the American period—which

Weavers have a number of options when it comes to wool, ranging from hand-spun to processed to commercially spun wool. They have a similar range of choices when it comes to color, including natural wool colors, vegetal dyes, aniline dyes (which can be used to mimic vegetal dye colors as well as provide bright colors), and finally, aniline dyed acrylic yarn. Most weavers have switched to processed yarn as they have found that when they weave with hand-spun yarn, they often are paid no more than when they use processed wool despite the enormous number of extra hours and the extra skill required.

began in 1848—when cowboys would pay as much as a month's wages for a good Navajo blanket. These blankets were favored for a range of uses, including, most importantly, as a bedroll and a rain slicker.

Many Navajo were imprisoned in 1864 for four years—after a long and brutal, no-holds-barred, scorched-earth campaign led by Kit Carson—at Ft. Sumner near Bosque Redondo on the hot dry plains of eastern New Mexico. There is no space here to recount their trials and tribulations except to cynically note that the reason for releasing them back to the homeland was that it was cheaper to let them support themselves.

A small band of Navajo had hidden out in Monument Valley during this period. Under the leadership of Hoskinini they had been maintaining livestock, notably sheep and horses, against the day the rest of the Navajo would return. This selfless foresight, coupled with Navajo resiliency, paid off.

SOCIAL CHANGE

The number of sheep held by the Navajo in 1869 was estimated at nearly 15,000 (the government had issued them Merino sheep—rather than their original churro sheep—upon their return, though the actual number they received

Woven by Rita White, this piece is based upon a First Phase Chief's blanket—the simple banded pattern that characterized most Navajo weaving for the first two centuries of Navajo wearing blankets. Highly prized Navajo blankets were actively sought by members of other tribes, ranging out onto the Plains among tribes like the Cheyenne. Early American visitors equated wealth with position and assumed that those who could afford to wear them must be chiefs—hence the name Chief's blanket.

Navajo textile arts are now the staple of business at Hubbell Trading Post. Some of the weavings reflect older patterns—many of which originated here a hundred years ago—while others show the continuing evolution of Navajo weaving art.

isn't certain), and by 1892 the number of sheep had swelled to 1,750,000! The wool market was strong as cotton production had been severely reduced by the Civil War and its aftermath. Unfortunately, 1892 was also the second year of a serious drought and was followed in 1893 with a financial panic Back East that devastated the wool market.

(The Navajo would again face the economic consequences of drought, overgrazing, and a bad national economy in the 1930s. It resulted in the Stock Reduction Act of 1933, and the subsequent slaughter of half a million Navajo livestock. Though designed to alleviate the problem of overgrazing and improve the quality of Navajo livestock, it was a Draconian measure and caused traumatic times for the Navajo people, especially since the U.S. government did not realize that the herds were the property of the women, *not* the men, essentially impoverishing many women and undermining a tenet of Navajo culture.)

In the midst of this social upheaval came another change for Navajo weaving. The first trading post, established at Fort Wingate the very year the Navajo were released from imprisonment, had been successful, and others applied for trading licenses. (There were roughly 40 by the turn of the century.) The traders sought protection from the fluctuating wool market by developing a market for Navajo-woven wool textiles for tourists who were beginning to travel to the West—often on the Santa Fe Railroad (it reached the western Navajo Reservation by 1881), staying at the renowned Harvey Houses. Navajo wearing blankets were rapidly disappearing in favor of new clothing fashions in the wake of Bosque Redondo. Navajo looms were not idle, however, for in addition to saddle blankets a new market had developed—for rugs as floor coverings.

Rugs during this era were generally bought and sold by the pound according to the grade. (Well into the 1900s traders recorded their rug sales not by the number of rugs sold, but by the tonnage.) In 1896 a basic Navajo saddle blanket, weighing between five and seven pounds on the average, sold for 35 cents per pound. What the weaver received can be placed in better perspective by comparing it to other commodities of the era. In comparing, things look grim: there was a time, in 1916, when goat skins were bringing more per pound than the average Navajo rug!

Since the late 1800s a number of traders have been credited with "saving" Navajo weaving from certain disappearance. These traders, along with outfits like the Fred Harvey Company, certainly deserve some credit, but it is credit that needs to be shared with the weavers themselves.

In more recent years a number of traders, and now collectors, have claimed to have discovered, re-discovered, introduced, or re-introduced the world to Navajo weaving. Most of these individuals deserve little if any credit, while the weavers, the creators of the fine textiles marketed and collected by others, deserve enormous recognition and credit for their perseverance, adaptability, skills, and artistic vision.

Germantown rugs are named for their commercially spun wool, which was used by some weavers from the 1880s to as late as the 1930s. Since the late 1980s there has been a revival of this colorful, often imaginative style, represented here by Cara Yazzie, who has "signed" her work by weaving a double-headed arrow in the upper right corner as her hallmark. Signed weavings are uncommon.

As among the Pueblos, missionaries introduced quilt making to the Navajo. Quilter Ann Tahbo is shown here with a quilt based on a Two Gray Hills rug pattern (which she stitched for her aunt) and another, of her own design, entitled "Guardian of the Field."

CATEGORIES OF NAVAJO WEAVING

Navajo weaving is categorized in many ways. From the standpoint of time, it is broken into four categories or periods: the *Classic Period* (1650-1865), the *Transitional Period* (1865-1895), the *Rug Period* (1895-1920), and the *Revival-Contemporary Period* (1920 to the present).

Before becoming too concerned about the periods and how to tell the difference between weavings of the various periods, consider the following: a Navajo woman who learned how to weave in the 1890s from a weaver who learned in the 1850s. She could still have been weaving—in the manner in which she learned—in the 1930s.

What if she wove a rug in the 1850s style in 1930...would it be Classic, Transitional, or Revival Period—and could anyone tell it was woven in 1930 and not 1850 if it were a classic dark brown and white banded blanket? The period dates, if not arbitrary, need to be thought of as fuzzy rather than precise and designed more to trace or define the evolution of Navajo weaving than to conclusively date a work.

Two-faced rugs are those woven with a completely different pattern on each side. They require a somewhat different loom set-up and considerable weaving skill. Most weavers create a geometric pattern on one side—like this twill weave—with a pictorial pattern on the reverse. Early ethnographers speculated as to whether it was done with a mirror or by two weavers working together. (It was a while before they actually asked a Navajo weaver how it was done!) This one was woven by Rosebell Wilson.

Pictorial rugs were once limited to trains, animals, and even words in a very flat, two-dimensional format. As landscapes became popular, weavers began to employ the same techniques of perspective that painters do, and sought to create more realistic images. A few Navajo textile artists weave so finely and skillfully that they are able to create what the eye sees as smooth curves, despite the rigid geometry of weaving, as in this fine example by Sarah Tso.

Lorenzo Hubbell actively encouraged weavers to produce textiles that he believed would sell faster and for a better price. This textile, woven in 1905, is an early example of the style he encouraged—Ganado Red.

The other way of categorizing Navajo weaving is by pattern. The earliest patterns were banded, with bordered patterns evolving during the early days of the trading post era. Many rug designs have names like Ganado, Two Gray Hills, Crystal, and Teec Nos Pos. Those patterns received their names because the designs first evolved in those regions. Regional styles did not arise until the 1920s and began to wane shortly after World War II when the Navajo population (like the rest of the country) became more mobile. A weaver in the Lukachukai area is as likely to weave a Ganado pattern as a weaver from Ganado. The last true regional style that developed was the Coal Mine Mesa Raised Outline, which developed immediately after World War II under the guidance of Ned Hatathli, director of the newly-founded Navajo Guild, who was from the Coal Mine Mesa area (now largely part of the Hopi Reservation) and related to a number of weavers in the area.

One of the more recent styles to develop is the Burntwater, known for its intricate patterning and use of many different colors. It is not uncommon for a Burntwater design to have 15 or more colors. These frequent changes require extra care and a highly refined sense of design so that the result is an overall pleasing effect rather than a jumble of colors and shape. This particularly fine example was woven by Jennie Slick.

Two-in-one and four-in-one rugs were woven in the past as novelties, but in the last decade weavers have begun to create complex "sampler" patterns like this Teec Nos Pos sampler by Cecelia George.

Not all patterns have names but regional styles were (and still can be) a competitive edge for traders, so attempts are still made to keep the practice alive. Some, like the Flagstaff rug and the Tuba City rug, not only never became established, but disappeared so quickly that no one remembers what they were supposed to look like. Other recent attempts have fared somewhat better, including Burntwater, New Lands (similar to Coal Mine Mesa Raised Outline weavings), and Dinnebito Black (similar to Ganados but with a little more black). More important than the name or lack of name for a pattern in a Navajo textile are the technical and aesthetic qualities of the weaving.

While Navajo textiles being woven today overall tend to be smaller than those woven 50 or more years ago, the quality of the weaving is better, with many falling into a tapestry category. This vegetal dye Wide Ruins style, by master textile artist Brenda Spencer, is an excellent example—from the fineness of the weave and intricacy of the design to the careful selection of the colors.

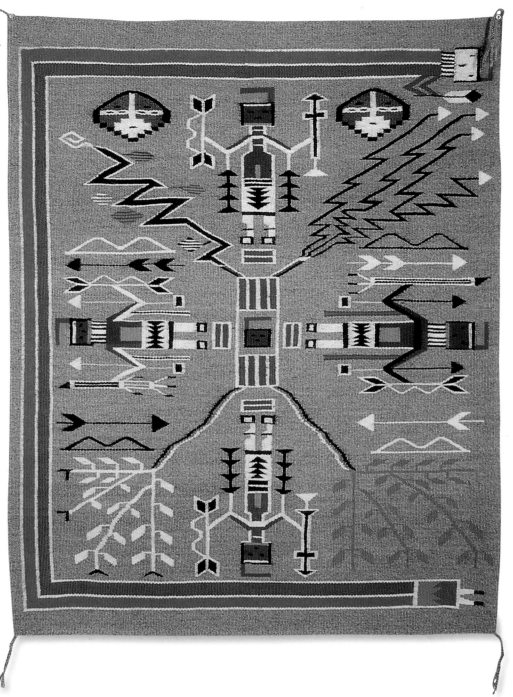

SANDPAINTING RUGS

Ye'ii, ye'ii bichaii, and sandpainting rugs are a style that, while associated closely with the Shiprock area, have been woven in many areas of the Navajo Reservation. Hosteen Klah is the best-known weaver of sandpainting rugs (along with two of his nieces), but he was not the first. The first recorded sandpainting rug was woven for a member of the Wetherill Expedition in the Chaco Canyon area in 1896. While there were no known repercussions for that weaver, the situation was quite different when Yanabah Simpson—the Navajo wife of trader Dick Simpson, who ran the Canyon Gallegos Trading Post southeast of Farmington, New Mexico—wove a rug with a ye'ii bichaii image shortly after the turn of the century.

Her work was proudly displayed in the trading post—to the immediate consternation of the Navajo clientele. Several Navajo men, including at least one *hatathli* (medicine man), were so incensed that Simpson had to immediately remove it from view, place it in his vault, and for a brief time is said to have feared that someone might set fire to the post. The rug sold a short time later to an East Coast collector for 300 dollars or more. The astounding sum was not lost on the Simpsons or other weavers in the area (which is still the center for ye'ii rugs) despite the dire warnings of the hatathli. Yanabah wove at least three more before she met a tragic end that fit one of the predictions of the hatathli: she died rather young in 1912.

In a rug of hand-spun wool, before the time-consuming task of weaving can begin, there are other, equally time-consuming tasks to be attended to: the wool must be spun, before it can be spun, it must be dyed (unless the weaver chooses to use the natural color of the wool), before it can be dyed the plants must be gathered—or the dye packets purchased from the store, and before it is dyed, it must be carded, which is what Effie Ben is doing here, closely watched by her nephew Daniel. But before she could begin carding, the wool had to be sheared and cleaned. Then there is the matter of maintaining the sheep herds....

ECONOMIC INFLUENCE

In recent years, to combat the time-intensive labor that results in an hourly wage usually below minimum wage, weavers have turned to commercially spun wool and processed wool. The former is ready to weave with while the latter—commercially cleaned, carded, spun, and dyed—still requires further spinning. Similarly, most weavers have turned to pre-dyed wool, the colors of which can match vegetal-dyed wool with precision. Rabbit brush and coffee remain the two most favored home dyes.

These practices are nothing new. Commercially spun wool—Saxony and later Germantown—was used as early as the 1850s, and aniline dyes were made available to Navajo weavers beginning in the 1870s, along with cotton string for the warp. The vegetal dyes we think of as traditional never numbered more than half a dozen colors until the 1940s when

Navajo weaver Nonabah Bryan cataloged 84 different plant dyes in a small pamphlet that is still in print today.

The 40-some weavers who participate in the Ramah Weaving Cooperative (RWC) are part of a group of weavers who are attempting to preserve and encourage the use of vegetal dyes as well as hand-spun wool. The higher prices for such textiles reflects the enormous amount of extra time and skill required. Such weavings come with certificates signed by the weaver attesting to the hand-spinning and listing the plants used in the dyeing process.

The RWC was formed with four goals in mind: promoting weaving, sheep husbandry, land protection, and community leadership. Churro sheep are the primary focus of the sheep husbandry. Churro sheep re-introduction has become the focus, in recent years, of several projects—

Prior to the 1930s, weavers relied on natural wool colors, aniline dyes, and only a few vegetal dyes. A Navajo teacher from the Fort Wingate School, Nonabah Bryan, tested and cataloged numerous vegetal dyes in the 1930-40s. Followed by the work of Mabel Myers, the number of available vegetal dyes numbers well over one hundred. Even so, many weavers prefer to use aniline dyes (first introduced by the DuPont company in the 1930s) because of the consistency of the color.

private for-profit, non-profit, cooperatives, tribal, and university-based. The churro were the sheep introduced by the Spanish. In the latter half of the 1800s, Americans introduced the Spanish Merino and then the French Rambouillet, preferred for their superior meat. Weavers generally found their wool greasier and more difficult to card and spin. Unfortunately, the quality of the reintroduced churro is uneven due to breeding difficulties.

(Text continues on page 28.)

Overleaf:
This almost rhythmic design of Navajo women was woven by Ardella Woody, whose grandmother, Della Woody, is well-known for similar work, but in a tapestry weave.

Many weavers prefer to focus their talents and time on the actual weaving, relying on the palette of colors offered by timesaving, commercially spun wool yarns that are widely available. Weavers whose masterpieces require a high warp and weft count will split these multiple-ply yarns into fine single ply strands. Others will take single ply yarns and re-spin them to create a finer, stronger yarn with which to weave.

Navajo textile artist Brenda Spencer learned weaving from her mother and now demonstrates the art for non Navajos. Her extra-fine weavings are achieved by repeatedly spinning commercial yarn to make it thinner and more uniform. The loom she uses is fundamentally the same as the ones her ancestors have used for many generations, but with improvements that make it easier to maintain the correct tension and weave a tapestry that meets the exacting standards of today's collectors.

Navajo master weaver Jennie Slick is shown here with one of her granddaughters watching closely. In Navajo culture watching quietly is the first step in learning, as it signals a readiness to learn, an interest in learning, and is proof positive of patience—the trait most necessary to acquire other skills. When a young woman spends the time needed to learn weaving with an elder relative, she learns more than just weaving skills— she learns the language and values of her culture. Weaving is key in the transmission of Navajo culture.

The real end product of all the weaver's work is to be seen and appreciated. When used on a floor, it is a useful item of beauty. When hung on the wall, it becomes an art piece to be seen and enjoyed every day.

WEAVING AS A LIFESTYLE

Weavers may weave consistently, or they may quit after they have learned the rudiments and made their first couple of weavings. Some may chose to weave rugs of a certain size and fineness that take no longer than a month to weave in order to have some sort of predictable income. Others have committed to weavings that took more than a year of hard work. One Navajo woman started her rug about the same time she began work on her master's degree. Both were finished the same month, and both now hang—framed side by side—in her home.

Many weavers sing weaving songs while they work—others prefer to listen to recorded music, and many offer a prayer to Spider Woman before a rug is begun and another after it is finished. Generally speaking, weaving is not an endeavor taken lightly. Many weavers will not work at the loom if troubled by unsettling thoughts or feelings. Something close to the state called *hozho* is the preferred frame of mind while weaving. *Hozho* encompasses the English notions of harmony, balance, beauty, and tranquility. It is said that a well-woven Navajo textile can transmit some of that feeling to a viewer.

This sandpainting design weaving, by Anita Tsosie, has a rainbow garland encircling and protecting the images, as is typical with actual ikaah or sandpaintings used in healing rites. What is unusual is that she has chosen to frame it within a series of encircling borders. The two figures at either side of the central ye'ii represent the Twin War Gods, dressed in their flint armor and wielding stone clubs. Most weavers of such images take pains to avoid exactly duplicating the traditional image. Here the weaver has given crooked lightning to both, while traditionally one would have crooked lightning as his weapon and the other straight lightning. The gods used these weapons to dispatch many of the enemies that were plaguing the Navajo people after they emerged into the new world.

Said one weaver, Ason Yellowhair, "I put a lot of thinking rug into it. Even at night, I think about how I'm going to weave."

Once a weaver has finished a rug, she will take it to sell. The long period of time required to weave demands that it be sold as quickly as is possible. Unless woven on special order, the weaver generally will take bids or offers from dealers until she receives an acceptable offer. Some may join with other weavers or drive into cities like Santa Fe, Phoenix, Albuquerque, or Tucson seeking a good market and better price. More rarely, they may hold it back for a special show or exhibition in hopes of selling it directly to a collector. Occasionally, they may send it to an auction like the well-known weavers' auction held regularly at Crownpoint, New Mexico, on the Navajo Reservation.

Still, weavers remember their work and recall the time spent before a loom. They often not only recognize their own work years later, but that of fellow weavers.

Weaver Loretta Benally has been quoted as saying, "I wish I could see them again. They are like my children. Wherever they might be, I hope they are bringing beauty into the lives of the people they are with."

This ye'ii rug was woven in the style of the very first ones that were made—nearly 100 years ago.

Basketry

Though the word weaving immediately conjures up images of Navajo textiles, basketry is another important weaving art among tribes of the Southwest. Such Indian basketry generally has been one of the more sought-after crafts. Beginning in the late 1800s, collectors began to avidly seek fine baskets and build extensive collections. Others, with less money and time to spend in pursuit of such objects, opted to weave them themselves. An organization called the Basket Fraternity sprung up to meet the needs of collectors and hobbyists alike. Using raffia, many hobbyists perused each new edition of the publication for Indian designs to copy. (Working patterns sold for 15 cents apiece.) These baskets often show up in older collections and are not infrequently mis-identified as Indian by people who try to identify them on pattern alone.

Prices for baskets today may seem high to those unaware of the hours and skill involved, but the finer baskets were never inexpensive. Baskets by the famed Paiute weaver Dat-so-lah-lee, which now bring 10,000 dollars and up depending primarily upon size and condition, brought up to 250 dollars even in the early 1900s—a time when a good monthly wage was less than 100 dollars.

The hours involved are such that it is rare for a weaver, even when selling directly to a collector, to earn minimum wage. Still, the love of the craft and the connection to one's heritage, combined with the demand among many tribes for Indian baskets to be used in religious observances, has kept the craft alive among several tribes, even while it has disappeared among many more. Using twining, twilling, coiling, and plaiting techniques, with tools as simple as an awl, a scraper,

The yucca coiled baskets (called poota *in Hopi) of Second Mesa, like this one being woven by Ernestine Dashee, have direct links in technique, materials, and even some design motifs, with those woven by their Puebloan ancestors over 2,000 years ago.*

The Western Apache bands of present-day Arizona were long-known for their finely woven, beautifully designed coiled willow baskets, a basketry tradition that is currently dormant. Burden baskets, however, continue to be woven as the twining technique, while demanding, is not as time-consuming as coiled basketry.

and perhaps a pair of nail scissors, Southwest Indian basketmakers continue their age-old craft. A small vanguard of weavers are now taking the craft into the realm of fine art.

Hopi Basketry

As with textiles, the Hopi are prolific weavers, but it is the women who weave baskets (though a couple of men do make plaited yucca baskets). Basket weaving at Hopi is not only generally segregated by sex, but by mesa as well. Coiled yucca baskets are made exclusively in the villages of Second Mesa, while willow wicker basketry is the province of women at Third Mesa. Utility baskets (like the plaited yucca sifters) and plain willow wicker work can be woven by weavers on any mesa, including First Mesa, which is the only mesa where women may make painted pottery. (These divisions undoubtedly contributed much to inter-village trade and relationships.)

Although less expensive baskets from the Tohono O'odham as well as from Mexico, Pakistan, and Africa are sometimes used in Hopi ceremonies like the *O'waqölt* or Basket Dance, where baskets are tossed to the crowd near the end, Hopi basket weaving owes much of its vitality to its use in many religious rituals. A small Hopi basketry plaque is given to a newborn at his or her first katsina dance. Cornmeal in many rituals is placed upon a basketry plaque—usually with prayer feather offerings. They are given during initiations into religious societies, and they are an important part of the wedding ritual: a large plaque is given to the man, whose mother or

Kevin Navasie demonstrates the final steps in finishing the rim of a Hopi yucca sifter basket. The ends of the yucca leaves are visible by each hand. These are not cut or trimmed until the basket has been completed. In Hopi these are called tutsaya. The geometric design was created with green unbleached and white bleached yucca, along with yucca that was dyed black. Aniline dyes are only occasionally used. In addition to geometric designs, artists have woven in katsina mask designs and words.

Janice Day demonstrates the splitting of yucca leaves using an awl. The thick middle must be trimmed away along with the sharp edges of the yucca leaf. These leaves will be plaited and then attached to a rim made of willow. In recent years metal rings have been used to make a more durable sifter.

This unusual example of basketry art was created by Bertha Wadsworth. It represents the Sa'lako katsina and has a wooden tablita or headdress and wooden feet.

This Hopi Angwusnasomtaqa or Crow Mother katsina is holding a yucca sifter basket (like the full-sized one in the background). During the Powamuy Ceremony in February, the Crow Mother katsina comes at first light into the village plaza holding a basket filled with prayer feathers.

Hopi willow wicker baskets were usually strictly utilitarian in nature, including such items as peach baskets, piki trays, carrying baskets, and cradleboards. This art basket by Ruby Chimerrica was woven with fresh willow that still had the leaves attached, with a narrow band of split willow near the neck of the basket.

33

This exceptionally large Hopi coiled basket, woven by Joyce Ann Saufkie, has a ring of Koyemsi *or Mudhead katsina faces around the rim, with an image of the Katsina Maiden or* Katsinamana *below, flanked by rain-cloud motifs. Most coiled Hopi baskets are typically between 10 and 12 inches across, but special ones may reach 2 feet or more in diameter. This one is about 30 inches.*

sister holds it for him for the rest of his life. When he dies, it is believed that this basket will speed his journey to the spirit world.

Baskets also form an important part of the wedding payback—when a bride must re-pay her relatives for her wedding robes and garments. The cost of the payback is considerable—if using wicker plaques she may need 50 or more, and for coiled plaques, a half dozen, but that includes one or two exceptionally large (and therefore exceptionally expensive) plaques. Those who are not weavers but make pottery usually trade their work for baskets. Others must find another trade or find the cash. In all, the Hopi themselves are perhaps the biggest customers for Hopi baskets.

These are examples of the Hopi willow wicker baskets woven in the villages on Third Mesa. One is woven in the shape of a Sa'lako katsina, two are utility baskets, and the other four are classic willow wicker plaques called yungyapu *in the Hopi language.*

This Hopi coiled yucca plaque, with a Crow Mother katsina flanked by four ears of corn and rain-cloud motifs around the rim, is one of the types of baskets used by Hopi women as "payback" for the woven robes they must have for their weddings.

Peggy Black is a Paiute basketry artist from the Douglas Mesa area of Utah. Here in her home, surrounded by the raw materials of her craft, she weaves baskets that range from the very traditional to the very contemporary—designs of her own artistic vision. She is one of a number of Paiute basketry artists working in natural and aniline-dyed willow, who are creating new traditions based on old traditions.

Navajo and Paiute Baskets

When many Navajo were forced into imprisonment at Ft. Sumner, a few bands were able to hide out in the Monument Valley area and in the canyons further northwest, among the Utes and Paiutes, with whom relations had often been poor. Necessity rapidly changed the situation and resulted in intermarriage between the groups. Paiutes, Utes, and Navajos make very similar baskets now. Some believe the Navajo learned from Paiutes, others that they learned from Pueblo weavers. Both are probably true as the Navajo were scattered into many bands across a wide swath of the northern region of the American Southwest.

Contemporary Navajo basketry is largely indistinguishable in appearance and technique from Paiute basketry. Paradoxically, many baskets identified as Navajo were in fact woven by San Juan Paiute weavers who lived on the Navajo Reservation. At the same time there was a belief that Navajo basket weaving was on the verge of disappearance. Instead, there was a group of very active weavers on Douglas Mesa, just northwest of Monument Valley.

According to the Navajo Creation Story, basket weaving was taught to them not by Spider Woman, but by Haashch'éé Yáti'i. He also showed them how to finish the rim coil with a herringbone pattern known as a false braid.

These fine willow baskets are examples of "story baskets" being woven by Navajo weavers in southeastern Utah. Encouraged by local traders and entrepreneurs, weavers are not only creating their own designs, but designs that grow out of a story or artistic vision of the artist.

Shanitl'ah, a woman of the Holy People, created or wove the first basket.

Navajo once made both utility baskets—including burden baskets, storage baskets, and coiled pitch-covered water jars called *tóshjeeh* (in English the name is a shortened version, *tus*, with a long "u")—and ceremonial baskets, but only the latter have survived.

THE WEDDING BASKET

Yts'aa is the name for the general type of shallow baskets still made today, but the so-called "wedding basket" is called *Alts'eeh*. It is used in

This Alts'eeh *is often called a wedding basket, but in fact is used in any number of different Navajo ceremonies (including weddings) to hold cornmeal used in blessings and prayers. This type of basket is made by both Paiute and Navajo weavers, and the pattern is sometimes used by Hopi weavers as well.*

These willow and sumac baskets show the range of patterns now being utilized by Paiute weavers. The basket in the back right is a Pima basketry design, while the back left is a new design created by a Paiute weaver.

the *Kinaalda* or puberty ceremony to hold corn cake, and in healing ceremonies to hold cornmeal for blessings. In weddings the basket is filled with corn mush and blessed with corn pollen by a maternal male relative of the bride. Bride and groom then share some of the food and pass it sunwise to guests. The basket is kept by the groom's mother.

The design of this ceremonial basket varies and is open to a number of different interpretations. The center can be earth, Mother Earth, the center of the world, or the place of emergence—or symbolize the beginning of life. The terraced motif is clouds or mountains. The number of terraces varies considerably, but some say that originally there were supposed to be 6 on the inside, representing either 6 sacred peaks or the 6 directions, with 12 on the outer side, after the number of ye'ii or Holy People. Others say the 12 are 12 songs or the 12 lunar months. The red band represents Mother Earth—or sun rays or a rainbow.

THE SPIRIT LINE

The *'atiin* (literally, pathway) we identify as a break in the design is the place of emergence or entranceway for spirits summoned in a healing ceremony. Some say the opening leads to all that is good—daily renewal with the sunrise. If there is no opening in the basket, the weaver "gets trapped inside." According to another taboo, failing to leave an *'atiin* in a ceremonial basket will cause the weaver to go blind.

A Navajo medicine woman, quoted in a basketry exhibit at the Navajo Museum in Window Rock, said, "The center is the beginning of life, moving outwards. Then the rain comes. These are the black clouds. The red designs are the reddish tinge in the sky and the dark mist. The outer white parts are the increase of the people. The pathway is to let the people emerge."

The center spot of a basket is like the whorls on fingertips, toe tips, and the hair on one's head—whorls through which the Holy Wind enters and breathes life into us.

This unusual basket in a horned lizard motif, was a joint effort—designed by Navajo artist Damian Jim and executed by Navajo weaver Sally Black.

INNOVATION

Much of the innovation in Paiute-Navajo basketry is happening in the Douglas Mesa area in Utah, not far from Monument Valley. It was here in these remote canyons claimed by the Paiute, that many Navajo hid from the army's attempt to capture and imprison them. Today, descendants of those Navajo and Paiute peoples are among the best weavers and include, most notably, the Rock, Black, and Bitsinnie families.

New styles and designs began to emerge in the mid- to late-1970s. Mary Holiday Black was, if not the first, then the most active and visible practitioner of the new Navajo basketry. In recognition of her work, she received a National Heritage Fellowship in 1995 at the White House.

Though earlier taboos against certain designs or the use of ye'ii images, or the need to leave an opening, no longer apply to non-traditional contemporary designs (that is, baskets which could not be used in ceremonies), many if not most of the ritual taboos or observances around the act of basketmaking still hold. Those prohibitions include:

- The weaver should not be touched while making a basket.
- Tie the sumac with yucca, not string.
- Never use a frayed basket.
- Leave frayed baskets in trees or under rocks (so sheep won't/can't get them).
- Put leftover material under a rock—do not burn.
- Don't wear a basket as a hat.

Navajo and Paiute basketry, often predicted to disappear along with Navajo textiles, continue to be woven and have evolved into craft art and fine art while maintaining ties to the past and the culture that nurtured their beginnings.

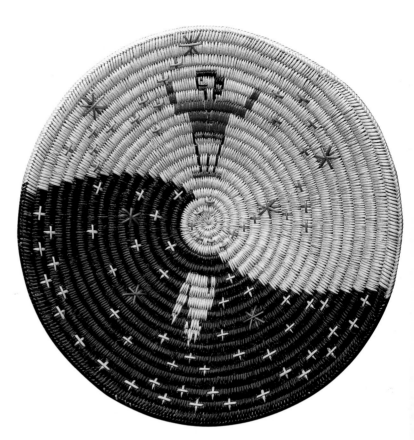

This Navajo "story basket" by Eleanor Black illustrates a tale from the Navajo Creation Story. The stars were being placed as constellations in the night sky. Coyote's help was refused because of his reputation as a bumbler and trickster. Not to be denied, he stole the stars—but he stumbled, the bag fell open, and the stars flew up willy-nilly.

Since the early 1990s Navajo artist Damian Jim has gained fame for creating basket and blanket designs on the computer. Often weavers collaborate with him, having him change colors or alter designs to suit their tastes and artistic vision before accepting the computer-designed special order. Surrounded by baskets and a weaving he designed, Jim exemplifies the Navajo tradition of borrowing, adopting and adapting new technologies, with the end result still being unmistakably rooted in an evolving Navajo tradition.

Apache Basketry

WHITE MOUNTAIN AND SAN CARLOS

Willow wicker burden baskets are the only surviving White Mountain and San Carlos Apache basketry type. The famed coiled willow baskets died out with the last active weaver less than 20 years ago. Burden baskets were traditionally used in gathering and carrying goods. Their long fringe (of buckskin or suede)—a fringe that was once tipped with dewclaws from the hooves of deer—distinguishes them.

The Apache live in mountainous regions, which are also the home to bears. Bears are not keen on surprises, and the noise those hoof tinklers made could alert a bear to their presence and avoid a potentially dangerous encounter. Since the late 1800s, metal has been used for the tinklers. They are now made in a variety of sizes, from miniatures suitable for use as earrings, to full-sized baskets—though functional tump straps, which stretched over the forehead for carrying, are no longer attached.

In recent years a story has started that the name comes from the fact that you are supposed to

Apache burden baskets generally had tinklers—whether of deer claws or metal—at the ends of the attached fringe. At one time, each band had their own variation in style, but over the past century stylistic differences have blurred.

Bright aniline dyes are a hallmark of Jicarilla basketry, though they fade over time.

The Jicarilla Apache Indians of northern New Mexico have a colorful, aniline-dyed willow basketry tradition that has been declared defunct more than once, yet weavers like Rowen Othole, Bertha Velarde, Loretta Romero, Nikkie Willie, and Adrella Venemo (work pictured here) have once again proven the pundits wrong, with a vigorous revival of Jicarilla basketry.

Here Jicarilla master weaver Molly Pesata teaches her daughter Ann, age 12, the art of weaving a willow basket, Jicarilla style. She weaves while Ann practices splitting willow. As with Navajo rug weaving, learning the craft takes time and ultimately involves learning about one's culture and traditions.

put your worries or burdens in the basket and the tinklers will sound to let you know that the wind has carried them away. A pretty story and useful to curio stores, but completely without foundation in Apache culture.

JICARILLA

Jicarilla Apache basketry has been officially declared dead or nearly gone more than once in the 1900s. It is currently undergoing yet another revival, largely through the efforts of the Pesata family. They use primarily vegetal dyes, though most Jicarilla baskets, going back at least to the early 1900s, use aniline dyes.

Woven of sumac or willow, these durable baskets last for years. Yet their designs often fade rapidly for a variety of reasons, including willow that was dyed while still green, long exposure to direct sun, and the use of aniline dyes that are highly susceptible to fading.

How this most recent revival of Jicarilla basketry will go is anyone's guess, but the example of the Paiute and Navajo art basket weavers indicates the potential for success.

This large basket by Jicarilla weaver Bertha Velarde recalls those woven in an earlier era and used as wastepaper baskets and clothes hampers. At least one weaver in the early 1900s even wove Jicarilla willow basketry fishing creels.

This Tohono O'odham basket employs both the covered-stitch and the split-stitch techniques. The split-stitch technique involves a more open stitching of the yucca over the green bear grass coil. The basket also showcases the traditional materials of *moho* or bear grass, white bleached yucca or *tokway*, *and black from the seed pod of the* ihuk *or devil's-claw plant. The Tohono O'odham weavers are the most prolific of the remaining basket-making tribes. Their work can often be seen in the religious ceremonies of other tribes, including the Hopi and many of the Rio Grande Pueblos in New Mexico.*

Tohono O'odham and Akimel O'odham (Pima) Baskets

The Tohono O'odham of the Sonoran Desert ("Desert People"—formerly known as the Papago) speak essentially the same language (a Uto-Aztecan language) as their relatives to the north, the Pima (Akimel O'odham, the "River People") who live along the Gila and lower Salt rivers. Traditionally, a Tohono O'odham *hoh* or basket is made from a coil of bear grass (*Nolina microcarpa*, called *moho* in their language) and sewn with bleached white yucca (*Yucca elata—tokway*). Other materials used include green or yellow-green unbleached yucca, black from the seed pod of the devil's-claw plant (*Martynia parviflora—ihuk*) and, on occasion, red from the root of the Spanish or shin dagger (*Yucca arizonica—oh'eetock*). There are two styles: the split-stitch, which is used for utility or storage baskets, and covered-stitch baskets for those which are subject to more wear, like baskets for parching or winnowing.

Generally, Pima baskets are woven of willow over a willow coil. However, intermarriage has always been commonplace and so you may see baskets woven in yucca by someone of Pima heritage and others woven in willow by a Tohono O'odham artist. O'odham—whether Tohono or Akimel—baskets woven in willow have become increasingly rare over the past half century to the point where only a bare handful of O'odham weavers are using willow.

ECONOMIC CHANGE

Due to the extreme lack of employment opportunities on the reservation, the number of Tohono O'odham who weave grows somewhat each year as does the number of baskets. Estimates of the number of current weavers (both those who weave regularly and those who weave

Though horsehair was long used for rope making, Tohono O'odham weavers did not begin using it as a basketry material until after World War II. Today horsehair baskets are among the finest woven and often sport highly intricate designs.

As part of an attempt to improve the prices weavers receive for their work and to ensure the continuance of the craft, the Tohono O'odham Community Action program sponsors a basket-weavers' association. Here members Geneva Ramon, Terrol Johnson, Rose Martin, and Sadie Marks display some of the baskets marketed by the association.

As with many of the other remaining basket-weaving tribes, some Tohono O'odham weavers are utilizing the designs of defunct basketry traditions in addition to their traditional motifs and new innovations based upon the weavers' artistic visions.

only occasionally) range between 300 and 500 (out of a population of some 18,000) and the best guess for the number of baskets woven annually for the last couple of years is 5,000 to 6,000—and that includes small split-stitch baskets and very simple tiny horsehair baskets.

While these weavings represent income for many families, the income is, with few exceptions, below minimum wage—well below it. The estimated hourly wage in the mid-1970s was about 20 to 25 cents an hour. By the late 1990s it had grown to roughly one dollar an hour. In an attempt to gain more respect—and better prices for their work, the Tohono O'odham Craft Association created the Tohono O'odham Basketweavers Association (TOBA) in 1997. Museum-related shows, exhibitions, and direct sales, as well as better publicity, are among the strategies being used. Additionally, a few weavers, notably Ruben Naranjo and Terrol Johnson, are creating baskets that have entered the realm of fine art.

Seri Basketry

The approximately 700 people who make up the Seri tribe live along the desert coast of the Sea of Cortez in Mexico. They call themselves *Comcáac*, which means "the people" in their language. Still fishermen, despite growing intrusion and competition from better-equipped non-Seri fishermen, the Seri still maintain their language and much of their tradition, including basketmaking. Long before there was an international boundary, the Seri and the O'odham peoples engaged in trade relations with each other in what we call the Greater Southwest.

Seri baskets are woven of *haat*, a large, almost treelike shrub called *torote* in Spanish, *limberbush* in English, and *Jatropha cuneata* in scientific jargon. This material, which must be gathered and processed prior to weaving, is used for both the coil and the stitching. The red-brown dye used comes from the inner part of the bark of the root of the white rattan plant, while the black used today is an aniline dye.

DAVID BURKHALTER

Seri weaver Angelita Torres with natural white and dyed red-brown torote *fibers at hand. Seri baskets are renowned for their strength and rigidity.*

A selection of Seri baskets, including a small hairbrush at the base of a large saptim *or storage basket. The basketry trays surrounding it are called* hasajáa.

DAVID BURKHALTER

Their baskets are well-regarded for workmanship, design, and sturdiness: rapping on the side of a good Seri basket is almost like rapping on a plank of wood. The largest Seri baskets, shaped like ollas or storage jars, are called *saptim* in their language. A year or more may go into the weaving of such a basket. One such basket, measuring 48 by 52 inches, required a year and a half of work. It is not surprising, then, that one expert estimates that only slightly more than a dozen such baskets have been woven in the past quarter of a century.

The completion of such a basket is the focus of a four-day ceremony that includes dancing, singing, feasting, and gifting.

As with other basket-making tribes, some Seri weavers are receiving requests to recreate designs from defunct basket-making traditions, from Yavapai Apache to Washo. Even so, traditional Seri designs and new innovations based upon those traditions, continue strong.

Rio Grande Pueblo Baskets

While coiled baskets were once woven in the Rio Grande pueblos, for well over a century, basket weaving has been very limited. At Jemez plaited yucca baskets are woven, and a few men at Santo Domingo Pueblo weave plain willow wicker baskets. Most of the Rio Grande pueblos rely upon Hopi, Tohono O'odham, or, occasionally, Jicarilla baskets, with imported baskets increasingly being used.

This willow wicker basket was woven by Andrew Harvier of Santa Clara Pueblo. Unlike at Hopi, among the Rio Grande pueblos it was common for men to weave baskets. Coiled basketry died out in the mid-1800s, leaving only willow wicker and plaited yucca sifters as the basketry styles.

Care of Weavings

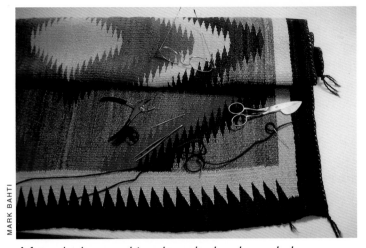

A frayed edge caught and repaired early can help avoid costly repairs later on. To properly repair a rug requires reweaving, not darning, and the skills in reweaving differ from the skills necessary to weave it. Most weavers do not repair textiles—that work is the province of specialists in textile restoration.

Properly cared for, a Navajo rug used on the floor can last for generations. If neglected—improperly stored, for example—insects can render it value-less within a matter of weeks. Much the same is true for baskets. Given how both can appreciate in value if the condition remains good, it is worth taking some precautions. One that is often over-looked is an appraisal. A competent appraisal should include a photograph and a detailed description that includes a coils per inch count for baskets and a warp and weft per inch count for Navajo textiles. These are important, objective gauges of the quality of the work

IMITATIONS

In the past several decades, copies of Navajo rugs have been woven in India, Pakistan (where copies of Navajo, Apache, and Hopi baskets are now being made), Belgium, Mexico and, more recently, Moldavia and the Ukraine. Each of these copies can be detected—though some are more difficult to detect than others—but one's best assurance is to buy from a reputable dealer who will state on the receipt that the textile you have purchased is Navajo made.

"Navajo design" and "Navajo style" have become code words for *not* Navajo made. Just because a weaving is identified as a Ganado, doesn't mean it is a Navajo-woven rug with a Ganado pattern. Similarly, "Indian made" does not necessarily mean *Navajo* Indian made, as there are Indian weavers in Mexico—some of whom are commissioned to use Navajo designs.

Don't jump to conclusions, and always get a written receipt fully describing the piece. Copies of Navajo weavings—if priced according-ly—have a place in the market and some may even be found in Indian homes, but they should *never* be sold in a manner that suggests that they are the true article. Most importantly, none of the copies will ever attain the value that a fine Navajo rug will.

CARE OF RUGS

A Navajo rug on the floor needs a carpet pad. The pad not only keeps the rug from sliding, but also provides a cushion between shoe heels and the hard floor. Make sure the pad runs right to the edges and corners so that foot traffic does not damage those areas by a "pinching" action. Replace the pad as needed—it's easier (and far less expensive!) than replacing the rug. The rug should be turned over and turned end for end periodically to even the wear and tear. No matter how much padding your rug has, don't place a piece of furniture on it as it will eventually wear a hole through the weaving.

The rug should be vacuumed regularly to prevent abrasive grit and sand from cutting the wool fibers. Do not use a vacuum with a beater attachment, and do not shake out a rug as the snapping action will eventually cause the strands of wool to break.

Keep the weaving free from moisture and don't hang it near a bathroom or spa area. If it becomes water-soaked, dry as fast as possible—you can use a wet vacuum or a fan, but do not use a hair drier as that will cause the wool to shrink. If the moisture is from anything other than water, blot it dry immediately. If there appears to be a stain, take it to a cleaner right then.

Dry cleaning removes vital oils (lanolin) from the wool, making the fibers brittle and more sus-

If a basket is heavily used, the stitches along the rim and base coils will suffer wear that causes them to fail, exposing the basket to more rapid deterioration. Less handling and an acid-free paper "coaster" under the basket will reduce wear.

ceptible to wear. Avoid steam cleaning as well, taking it instead to someone who has experience hand-washing fine Oriental or Navajo textiles, as both weaving types require similar care.

If the rug is to be hung, the very best way to hang it is with Velcro©. The hook side of the Velcro© is attached to the wall or a strip of wood that is then attached to the wall. Then simply press the rug against it, and the hook side will grip the fibers of the rug. Rugs that have been used on the floor for some length of time may not have enough nap or fuzziness left in the fibers to be held this way.

In those cases a decorative wooden clamp, with Velcro© to help cushion the pressure, is the best system. As with rugs displayed on the floor, reverse and turn end for end the rugs you hang so that any fading is minimized and distributed over both sides. Done a few times a year, along with a light vacuuming of both the textile and the wall, it helps to discourage wool-eating insects, which don't like the activity. Professional mothproofing is highly recommended. Crickets, clothes moths, silverfish, and carpet beetles—also known as Buffalo bugs/moths—are the most common pests. If you are not keen on regular mothproofing, then the alternative is to vacuum the rug and the wall behind it monthly, without fail.

When storing a rug for any length of time, have it cleaned, moth-proofed, and then rolled up with a light sprinkling of para-dicholorobenzine moth crystals. While some use plastic bags, most serious collectors will wrap them in acid-free paper or a cotton sheet and seal the edges with tape. A cedar chest may help keep rodents from getting to the rug, but do not count on cedar chests or closets to provide sufficient protection.

CARE OF BASKETS

The strength and durability of Indian basketry is determined by its materials and the quality of the weave. Yucca does not wear as well as willow and it is more porous—therefore more susceptible to staining. On the plus side, yucca fiber baskets are easier to repair. Qualified restorers of baskets are even harder to locate than qualified rug restorers, so you would do well to be especially vigilant of your fine baskets.

Avoid direct sunlight and extreme moisture or extreme dryness. Particularly as they age, baskets will readily absorb soaps and oils, so exercise care in handling them and do not hang them in or near cooking areas. If you are going to use a basket for holding objects—whether cookies or keys—line it with a cloth napkin and make sure you do not overload the basket or it will rapidly break down the fibers and thus the strength and shape of the basket. When hanging, use natural white thread or a lightweight stainless or galvanized wire. Find two openings between the warp and weft to slide the ends of the wire or thread through and tie them off in back. Be sure you position the loop above center so that the basket hangs as flat as possible. This will prevent the basket from losing its shape and eventually "flopping" forward.

The fibers are organic so you must expect some degree of darkening of the lighter colored fibers and fading of the colors. The fibers will lose some of the flexibility with age. To combat this drying, some people attempt to "revitalize" the fibers with products ranging from mineral oil to baby oil, neither of which I recommend. If you must, the best mixture to use is a 50-50 mix of rubbing alcohol and pure glycerin. The best thing to do is simply retire the basket from use and handling.

As with textiles, baskets are vulnerable to bugs. Vigilance is your best protection as fumigating, while effective, deposits an oily film on the surface of the basket. To eliminate an infestation you can wrap up mothballs in cloth, place them on the basket, and wrap the basket in a black plastic bag. Set it somewhere warm for a few days, then remove and air the basket. Another option is to use the freezing service that many pest control companies offer.

The balls of yarn in Jennie Slick's basket can be thought of as all the diverse influences—Pueblo weaving technique, Spanish sheep, American aniline dyes—that have been absorbed into an important symbol of Navajo culture.

SUGGESTED READING

DALRYMPLE, LARRY. *Indian Basketmakers of the Southwest*. Santa Fe, New Mexico: Museum of New Mexico Press, 2000.

DEDERA, DON. *Navajo Rugs—How to Find, Evaluate, Buy, and Care for Them*. Flagstaff, Arizona: Northland Press, 1996.

DEWALD, TERRY. *The Papago Indians and Their Basketry*. Tucson, Arizona: Self-Published, 1979.

HEDLUND, ANNE LANE. "Contemporary Navajo Weavings— Thoughts That Count," *Plateau Magazine*, Vol. 65, No. 1. Flagstaff, Arizona: Museum of Northern Arizona, 1994.

KENT, KATE PECK. *Navajo Weaving: Three Centuries of Change*. Santa Fe, New Mexico: School of American Research Press, 1985.

MAULDIN, BARBARA. *Traditions in Transition*. Santa Fe, New Mexico: Museum of New Mexico Press, 1984.

MAXWELL, GILBERT, Revised Edition by BILL and SANDE BOBB. *Navajo Rugs: Past, Present and Future*. Santa Fe, New Mexico: Heritage Art, Ltd., 1984.

MCMANIS, KENT and ROBERT JEFFRIES. *A Guide to Navajo Weavings*. Tucson, Arizona: Rio Nuevo Publishers, 1999.

TEAGUE, LYNN S. *Textiles in Southwestern Prehistory*. Albuquerque: University of New Mexico Press, 1998.

Inside back cover: The future of Navajo textiles is as strong and full of promise as the visions of the newest generation of Navajo weaving artists. Here Charlene Ben, age 13, is becoming a part of that future.

Back cover: Though sometimes referred to simply as Germantown Revivals, they are much more: they are new explorations of an old tradition by Navajo textile artists.

KC Publications has been the leading publisher of colorful, interpretive books about National Park areas, public lands, Indian lands, and related subjects for over 37 years. We have 5 active series—over 125 titles—with Translation Packages in up to 8 languages for over half the areas we cover. Write, call, or visit our web site for our full-color catalog.

Books on Indian Culture and the Southwest: Southwestern Indian Arts and Crafts, Southwestern Indian Tribes, Southwestern Indian Ceremonials, Southwestern Indian Pottery, Southwestern Indian Weaving, I Is for Indians, Canyon de Chelly, Monument Valley, Mesa Verde, Grand Circle Adventure, The Rocks Begin to Speak, The Southern Paiutes, The Navajo Treaty, Zuni Fetishes. A hardbound edition combining the first 3 Southwestern Indian books is also available.

To receive our full-color catalog featuring over 125 titles—Books, Calendars, Screen Scenes, Videos, Audio Tapes, and other related specialty products:

Call (800-626-9673), fax (702-433-3420), write to the address below,
 Or visit our web site at www.kcpublications.com

Published by KC Publications, 3245 E. Patrick Ln., Suite A, Las Vegas, NV 89120.

Created, Designed, and Published in the U.S.A.
Printed by Tien Wah Press (Pte.) Ltd, Singapore
Color Separations by United Graphic Pte. Ltd